Eight Tomatoes

Letters from the Heart

That Heal, Fulfill & Forgive

Brenda, I think you + everyone can find something important in these pages.
Ken

Kenneth C. Mitchell

Seagull Press • Springfield, Illinois

Seagull Press Publishing Company
Post Office Box 9203 Springfield, IL 62791 (217) 787-7100

Copyright © 2020 by Kenneth C. Mitchell

All rights reserved. No part of this publication may be reproduced, stored in a retrieval system or transmitted in any form or by any means electronic, mechanical, photocopying, recording or otherwise without the prior written permission of the author or publisher.

For information about special discounts for bulk purchases, please contact Seagull Press Special Sales at 217-787-7100.

None of the information, suggestions or stories in this book should be construed as medical advice.

ISBN 978-0-578-74729-3
Library of Congress Control Number: 2020946941
First Printing: October 2020
Printed in the United States of America
Cover by Tony Sanguedolce of Dolce Design
Illustrations by Joey Dodd
Formatting by Capitol Blue Printing, Springfield, IL

to Anne

Contents

Acknowledgements

Foreword by Dr. Tom Hill

Introduction……………………………………………………*1*

Part 1   CHANCE MEETINGS

    1. The Farmer…………………………………*5*
    2. The Doctor…………………………………..*13*

Part 2   CHERISHED LETTERS

    3. A Varity of Letters………………………...*23*
    4. Specialty Letters……………………......*31*

Part 3   CRAFTING YOUR LETTER

    5.   The Style………………………………..*41*

    6.   The Guidelines……………………….*47*

    7.   The Presentation…………………………..*55*

Part 4   YOUR IMPACT

    8.   Changing the World..………………….....*61*

    9.   Bringing Families Together……………....*63*

   10. Brightening Your Star………………..……*67*

Part 5   THE REST OF THE STORY

   11. The Miracle…………………………...……*73*

   12. The Mystery…………………………...…*77*

Conclusion………………………………………..…*81*

Author's Note……………………………………….*83*

Appendix……………………………………………...*85*

About the Author………………………………………*131*

Acknowledgements

Many thanks to my editorial staff who looked over the manuscript:

Marcia Bullard, Nancy Goble, Lindsay Teefey, Sue Mitchell, Karen Kelly, Virginia Scott, Ladd Mitchell, Jerry Tansky, Chaz Bordeau, Sue Maxwell, Ray and Pam Bruzan, Steve Rambach, Bob Givens, Sandy Utterback, Katie Fitzgerald, Donna Galassi, Karl Reed, Vicky Whitaker, Beccie Galloway, Linda Brissenden, Karen Birnbaum, and Deb Huffman.

These friends contributed ideas and corrections that have greatly added to the book.

Several other friends offered personal letters so I could illustrate some of the variety of Tomato Letters in the back of the book. I have changed the names and made most of them anonymous.

Major thanks to my cover designer, Tony Sanguedolce, who has worked his magic on several of my other books and continues to in this one. And to a new member of our book publishing efforts, the talented illustrator, Joey Dodd. He also provided the picture of the basket of tomatoes on the front cover.

Foreword

When my friend Ken Mitchell sent me a copy of his latest book, *Eight Tomatoes*, I thought to myself, "Well, this is different!"

In addition to being different, this book contains the four ingredients that make books really stand out according to many publishers: a meaningful message, passion, universality, and a great story. This book has all of these.

I embrace Ken's message of taking the time to send close friends and loved ones letters that tell them how much you truly care about them, acknowledge their accomplishments, give them encouragement—and the rest of the feelings expressed in the letters in this book.

Ken is obviously passionate about the idea of writing these special letters. You can feel that passion on every page. And it has certainly carried over to me, and I hope it will carry over to you, too.

Heart-to-heart thoughts and feelings and those emotional connections that bind us together are the universal and the timeless in us all. When it comes down to it, what else really matters? And that is what Ken urges us to send, in letter form, to those important to us in our lives.

And what captures our imagination and interest more in a book than a real story, a narrative that rings true? Meeting two people out of the blue— the basis for this book—causes me to conclude that these were not chance meetings at all. Those make up the best story of them all, as you will soon discover.

I believe that *Eight Tomatoes* is inspiring, uplifting and will make your heart sing, as it did mine. And, if you're like me, it will encourage you to sit down and compose letters to the most significant people in your life.

DR. TOM HILL,
Founder and CEO, Eagle Goal Coach

Eight Tomatoes

Introduction

As I slice my tomatoes for lunch these days, I usually think back on the eight tomatoes that I received as a gift from an old doctor many years ago. Thinking about those tomatoes also reminds me of the letters that I have written from that chance meeting with him and a farmer three years before him.

I followed the advice I myself gave to the sad doctor and wrote my own letters to my wife, my four sons, my mother, and my daughter.

This book was kept short so you can read much of it while waiting for a hair appointment, a doctor's visit, or during some other morsel of time in your day. It is intended to get you to think about writing your own "Tomato Letters" to your loved ones and others you care about.

These two men whom I serendipitously ran into form the foundation for this true story. They are similar in that they wrote heart-to-heart letters to their loved ones and touched lives in uncommon ways.

Here's hoping these two stories will prompt you to be open to your own letter-writing. If you do take on this challenge, please do it right away, without delay. You never know when one of us will be light-beamed off the planet.

Part One

Chance Meetings

Chapter 1

The Farmer

Doctors heal people and sometimes ordinary people do too. But it all started with the farmer.

I'd been selling long-term care plans for several years, and my enthusiasm had been waning lately. Still, I did well in that career because I believed in the cause—that I was saving families from financial devastation, family disruption and stress that several years of long-term care can bring down on them.

On a blustery winter morning as I drove to an appointment near rural Blue Mound, a small town in the heart of Illinois, I was wondering why I was still in this business. My usual run in the selling industry was about a half-dozen years for a particular product. After that I needed a new challenge. Then a flash of insight answered that question: Maybe I'm still in this business because I'm supposed to meet somebody special, a bit of serendipity that was a common occurrence in my life.

I've always felt we come into contact with people for a purpose, a special reason, that there is some sort of divine order to every daily experience. Whether universally true or not, that day more than 20 years ago proved that feeling to be true for me.

A ruddy-faced retired farmer answered his door and invited me in. He motioned me toward the couch in his living room and asked if I wanted a cup of tea. As we drank the tea, he listened as I went through my introduction, saying how I got into the business and how our visit might help him and his family.

The next part of the ice-breaker conversation was asking him about his family. He quietly, almost in a whisper, told me what I wasn't prepared to hear. His wife had recently passed away from some illness I can't recall, probably cancer. He told me almost more than I wanted to hear about his loss and all of a sudden he stood up straight and said, "Ken, would you please wait a minute? I want to show you something."

He turned around and walked down the hall into a bedroom. As I waited for him, I rose to look around the room to gaze at the family pictures. I saw one of him and his wife taken many years ago when they looked very young, maybe around the time they were married.

The farmer came back within a minute or two and held out a paper that he asked me to read. It was two pages—front and back—typed and double-spaced. I started to glance at it and speed-read it to get the gist of it. However, I soon could tell it wasn't the kind of letter to skim. I turned it over and saw his signature at the bottom. It was a letter to his wife.

I looked up and asked him, "Do you mind if I take a few minutes to read this carefully? It seems interesting." He nodded. As I leaned back on the couch, he sat down too, crossing his legs in his chair.

It was the most personal of letters and, as I read it slowly, I wondered, *Why would he bring me so intimately into his world?*

I'm a slow reader, and it took me several minutes to finish it. When I was done, I looked up at the farmer, and he continued, "My wife and I were married for many years, and she was my closest friend. We had three children—all grown and out of the nest—so we had been even closer the last several years. She was sick for quite a while, and I took care of her here at the house. She died a month ago, and it's been tough."

He took a deep breath and then explained the letter.

"After she passed, I wanted to tell her in a thoughtful way what she had meant to me. So, I sat down and started to write. It took me a morning—at the kitchen table, over there—to put it all down. I'm not much of a writer, but after some starts and stops, I got it down. I then typed it out, like you see it.

"Ken, that's forty years of feelings, there and, by gosh, I think I got 'em down pretty well. I made some copies and passed them around to family and friends to show them how I felt about her."

I didn't know what to say—an odd loss of words for a man whose job required them. I processed what he said, still holding the letter in my hand. Finally, I asked him if I could have a copy. I explained that I send a newsletter to my clients periodically and would like to include it in the next one. He was more than happy to let me have one.

He talked quietly about his wife. He needed to talk, and I suppose I needed to listen. The essence of that one letter was such a loving summary of what he and she had meant to each other. He told me how her departure left a hole in his life. The fact that he wasn't farming anymore added to that sense of despair.

I don't think I said anything, I just sat there with him. It was obvious there would be no insurance selling that morning. He wasn't in that frame of mind and neither was I. My purpose was to be a stranger converted to a friend and take it all in. After a half hour, he and I said our goodbyes. I thanked him for the letter and left. I never saw him after that, although I thought a lot about him and that letter over the next number of months and years.

I drove to my next appointment and couldn't get him or that letter out of my mind. It changed my mood to a pensive one, and I don't think I was very effective with my other appointments that day.

What I do remember, as if it were yesterday, is what I was thinking as I drove around the rest of that day. I kept thinking, *Wouldn't it have been nice if he had written that letter to her while she was alive? And, wouldn't it have been wonderful if she had written him one in exchange?* That's not to minimize the significance of his letter at all for it brought him much comfort and closure.

But, if they had exchanged letters, they could have shared those deep feelings in a different way. I'm sure they talked a lot about how they loved each other, but, in my mind, that farmer could be holding on to her letter and reading and rereading it—an enduring gift that would keep on giving, especially in his darkest hours. And, what treasure those two letters would have been for their children and their children, and on and on down the line.

Chapter 2

The Doctor

Every once in a while I pondered that letter and again wished the farmer and his wife had written letters to each other before her passing. I don't know why it stuck in my mind. In hindsight, I suppose it was germinating into something useful when I would meet another intimate stranger. On a sunny spring morning three years later, I met that other stranger.

He had sent in a card for information on my insurance plan, and I was at his doorstep for our appointment.

He was slightly stooped and wore a shock of gray hair and a kindly smile. I knew from my notes he was 84.

He led me into his living room and asked me to sit on the sofa while he put himself in a recliner across the coffee table from me. He looked me over intently as he asked me questions, the reverse of how I wanted to begin an interview. I eventually started as I always did, with questions about his family, work and interests. I was, however, stopped cold once he began describing his family situation.

He shared with me that he was a retired physician originally from "the old country," and when he said that I thought of my own grandfather who used that phrase repeatedly as I was growing up down the street from my Italian grandparents. I was also suddenly struck by the similarity in physical features between the doctor and my grandpa. He explained, as if it were a confessional, that he had been an autocratic father and husband, which, he said, "I had unfortunately learned from my own father and grandfather back in Lithuania."

In a contrite tone, he admitted he was so strong and inflexible that he eventually drove his wife and two sons away some years ago. He gave me several examples of how distant he was to all of them and wished now, in his twilight years, that he had put his ego away and shown kindness instead of authority and superiority.

Then he asked me a question that stunned me to my core. In a sincere and kind way, he asked, "What would you do to make amends with them, if you were me?"

He stared at me without saying anything else for maybe a half minute, his look resembling a plea more than anything else. For some reason I thought back to that farmer's loving letter.

Surprised at first, I collected my thoughts and responded, "Doctor, here's what I would do. I would write each a letter explaining in detail how you now feel and how you wish you could take back those harmful things you said to them."

Without hesitation, leaning toward me from his chair, he asked, "Would you help me with it?" I said I would and then, without understanding exactly what or how I would do it, I continued, "Wait about a half an hour or so. I've got to run home and get something for you. Don't leave. I'll be right back." I left my briefcase and headed home, just ten minutes away.

When I arrived home, I sat down at my computer and started typing. I was laying down a list of ideas to incorporate into such a "love letter" as I called it. I don't think it took me fifteen minutes to write non-stop two full pages of talking points that I called "guidelines." It's as if the words just fell onto the pages— dictated by some unseen power.

As I drove back to his duplex, I tried to figure out how I was able to write precise ideas with no hesitation or mistakes without so much as a note card. I must have had them organized and packed in some part of my brain during those three years since my visit to the farmer's home. *Strange*, I thought.

If I remember correctly, I didn't even knock when I walked back up the steps to the doctor's door. I stepped in and nodded to the doctor, who was waiting for me, and sat back down on the couch. He was sitting in the same chair he was in when I left. I then explained to him about writing three letters.

"Doctor, I would write three separate letters and use these guidelines in each. Write from your heart and go down this list. Explain to them how you feel about each one of them. The key is to explain your feelings and don't try to rationalize why you acted and spoke to them like you had in that other life. The most important thing is not to be critical. Everything should be positive. It's about contrition, Doctor, saying you're sorry about your past behavior and wanting to make amends."

He looked at me reassuringly and seemed to get what I said. I emphasized that I would leave the guidelines with him and suggested he follow them to the "T."

I continued and said, "Also, transcribe the final draft onto some really nice paper." I mentioned, as an example, fancy stationery (made of banana leaves and stems pressed together) I just received from my company as an incentive gift to win a trip to Costa Rica that year. The unique paper was beautiful—rough textured with matching envelopes.

He then seemed unsure of himself and asked, "Ken, would you help me write it? We can sit down and do it right now." Here was a medical professional—a psychiatrist, no less—asking an insurance man to help *him* form his thoughts into coherent letters. I declined and explained myself as sensitively as I could.

"Doctor, I feel this is your project. You have all this baggage in you, and you need to get it out yourself. It will take an hour or two to write each letter and then there's revising to do. Once you get them done, set them aside for a couple of days and let everything settle. Then go back and review them and make any last-minute improvements. Finally, write them in your own hand on some fancy stationery as I mentioned.

When you get done with the drafts, if you want, give me a call and I will be happy to look them over and give suggestions if they're needed. However, what you are writing is highly personal and you probably will want to keep the letters private."

He seemed all right at that point about writing them by himself. He thanked me for my time and help and invited me to "walk out back with me and look at my garden for a minute." That again reminded me of my grandfather who also had a beautiful kitchen garden in his backyard every summer.

I didn't get a sale from him that day, but he did give me a brown bag of big, ripe tomatoes. When I arrived home, I washed them, put them in a wicker basket on our table, and spent several minutes admiring them. Each of the eight tomatoes was perfectly formed and looked delectable. I thought to myself, "Well, Doc, you didn't buy any insurance, but you gave me a wonderful gift." Between my wife and me, those eight tomatoes were gone within a couple of days.

Part Two

Cherished Letters

Chapter 3

A Variety of Letters

After rereading that farmer's letter to his departed wife and the letter guidelines for the doctor, I decided to categorize what I first called love letters or appreciation letters as to their primary purposes. The farmer's letter I call a Last Letter or Saying Good-bye Letter. The doctor's letter I call an Apology Letter, Asking for Forgiveness, or I'm Sorry Letter.

This chapter will describe the eight basic Tomato Letters I eventually came up with. When you write your own letters, you can pick whatever letter aligns with your purpose, combine them, or think of your own categories.

They are yours to construct any way you want. Taking the farmer's example, it is also appropriate to write letters to departed friends and relatives. After all, one of the central functions of any of these missives is to make you, the writer, feel better for having expressed your feelings.

Other purposes of these letters include precious gifts to someone you care about, edifying a person, encouraging and even memorializing them.

Appreciation/Gratitude/Congratulations Letter This could be acknowledging someone in a high-risk job, such as a grocery store clerk in the current pandemic crisis, congratulating someone completing a college program, or other difficult project or task. A relative may have achieved or overcome something important, such as a sickness or divorce. It could be for being a good person, something you've never mentioned to them before. (An example letter in the Appendix is from a father to his son, praising him for persevering as a medical student among other things. Each of the letters in this and the following chapter will have examples in the back of the book.)

Love Letter This is a traditional letter we usually think about when writing a loved one who is away, or someone you are dating, or in a serious romantic relationship. Many of us have sent such letters to a parent or to someone we are dating or married to. In a sense, our farmer was writing such a letter to his wife, expressing not only his love for her, but mentioning important milestones they shared during their long life together. I wish I still had his letter, but it was somehow lost among my business papers.

<u>Forgiving Letter</u> This is a hard letter to write because someone (probably close to us) wronged or harmed us. We may have had this stuck in our craw for years, festering. And, now it is time to tell them we forgive them. I once had a tenant farmer steal grain from me. When I called him on it, he laughed and said I could never prove it, which was true. I forgave him in my mind, although I didn't even think of writing him back then. I forgave him shortly afterwards because I became aware that holding that grudge would hurt me and fester in me. I even said hello to him when I would see him on the street, although he would put his head down and walk past me without a word. Because of the sensitivity of such a letter, you may even write it and then stick it in a drawer somewhere or even burn it. Your job, after all, is done once you write it, and you can close the matter in your mind and heart.

<u>Apology/Asking for Forgiveness/I'm Sorry Letter</u>
In some ways, this may be even a harder letter to write because it was you or I who did the offending. There are many classic examples of this. One that comes to mind in my life is about a friend in the farm community where I lived for several years. He had been most helpful to me on my farm on many occasions. Yet, when it came time for him to have a farm sale, I did not show up to help him as did our other friends. My excuse was that it was too sad an affair since his landlord had taken away his tenancy. But that was a cop-out, and I should have helped. I have just recently written to him after all these many years. Remember, it is much better late than never.

<u>Thank-You Letter</u> This heartfelt letter can be for anything from thanking a person for being a good friend over the years to thanking one for a particular act of kindness, such as a gift. For example, I have sent letters to former teachers thanking them for being wonderful as teachers. The same goes for a mentor or trainer. I once received a financial gift to pay for printing a book. I sent a letter to my benefactor for the act of kindness that was totally unexpected. I have a friend who had a health crisis, and I suggested to him to send letters to two people who indirectly saved his life.

Sympathy/Condolence Letter As with all these examples of letters, there are many instances when such a sympathy letter is appropriate. They range from a close friend losing a loved one to another person losing a job or someone having a financial crisis. You can also send a letter to a relative who has a serious health challenge and offer help in the process.

Advising Letter This kind of letter might be sent to a friend who is going through a struggle you personally experienced. For example, after a divorce, I drove out to California thinking a new location would make things better. If a friend was considering a similar avenue, I might write him a letter explaining how I finally coped with that profound personal experience. Sometimes it is more poignant to take the time and write a person a well-thought-out advice letter, instead of having a conversation. Another type of advising letter is recommending a friend, relative, or student for a job or to a school.

The Last Letter/Saying Goodbye Letter This is the farmer's letter. Shortly after I suggested to the doctor to write his letters, I decided to write each of my four boys plus my wife and mother. Not at all an apology letter genre, those were instead special letters telling them how much I loved them, asking them to forgive any of my shortcomings, and sharing how proud I was of them for a variety of reasons. It was two pages, the length I recommend for most letters, so it can be read in 10 minutes or less. In addition to telling them how much you love them, this type of letter can be kept as a treasured gift for their entire lives. Over the years I have revised the letters to my loved ones and placed them in my beneficiary notebook to be read when I pass.

Chapter 4

Specialty Letters

There is another class of letters which I call specialty letters that you might want to consider. These are some of my favorites. Here is the description of the eight letters in this specialty category. The full number of such letters is limited by your imagination.

<u>Angel Letter</u> This is one that you write on behalf of your guardian angel to another person's guardian angel or from your angel to the person themselves to ask for help on a specific issue. Here's an example. A friend of mine told me that her contractor would not come back to

finish his work in her house. She tried everything, including phone calls and letters, but he would not return to complete her home project. She couldn't figure out what the problem was. I suggested she write a letter to his guardian angel from her guardian angel. She is the kind of person who is open to new things, so she took me up on it. She composed the letter and then placed it in her top drawer and waited. In a couple of weeks, she excitedly told me he had recently come over and finished the job as though nothing had happened. (Doubt it enough to try it!)

<u>Letter to God</u> It eliminates any middle people, even angelic beings. Going directly to the Source is sometimes the most efficient way to handle a request.

<u>Letter to Your Future Family</u> This one introduces yourself and gives advice is another technique I've used. By future family I am referring to your descendants down the way, perhaps several generations. Don't you wish you had a letter written by a long-dead relative, say from the early 19th century, wishing you good luck, offering advice, or describing their life? Some people have these in the form of old diaries, but yours will be a direct, first- person communication to them. These letters would be cherished as family heirlooms.

<u>Letter to a Child</u> He or she could either be alive or may have passed. No letter would be more precious than this one. Similar to the farmer's letter, it can be a way to talk with your dear child as he did with his beloved wife. It may resolve issues, say goodbye, or in other ways reach closure. It may be merely a thank-you letter, congratulations, or any other of the basic types of letters. Children bring out the sincerest emotions in our lives, and these letters may be even more meaningful when the child reaches maturity and reads it with different eyes.

<u>Letter to Deceased Relatives or Friends</u> This could be by sharing, thanking, apologizing, etc. Again, this is what the farmer did for his wife. In addition to children who may have passed, as we described above, these letters take into account spouses, parents, grandparents, etc. I have an old, faded picture of my grandfather with his parents and siblings, staring at us through the mists of time. Since he died just two months after I was born, I never had a chance to meet him. After having researched his life for my father's biography, I took that opportunity to write him in his afterlife. I also wrote a dear friend, whose closeness faded throughout the years which I felt terribly bad about.

<u>Time-release Letter</u> It could be a letter to a child, brother or sister, or another person you love dearly at important future times in their lives, such as birthdays, anniversaries, graduations, weddings. Perhaps you have a serious disease that will claim your life in a few months or a year. (Or, there is such a time gap in your ages that you will not be around for most of his or her life.) You see this theme played out in movies and news reports every once in a while. What a nice surprise when your loved one begins to receive these by way of a relative, a bank trust, etc.

<u>Letter to Yourself</u> This could prove to be the most important letters. It is often said that we truly can't forgive others until we forgive ourselves. We can be far too critical of our own actions that prevent us from our good. There are variations to these letters as there are to most of the others. For example, you can write to your higher self or to your guardian angels on behalf of yourself. A common theme to your self might be forgiving yourself for troublesome habits, addictions, etc., that caused problems for you and others. It can be a powerful catharsis, especially if you've tried everything else.

<u>Unexpected Letter</u> When you place yourself in this letter-writing mindset, wonderful, unexpected miracles can happen. For instance, *you* might receive a letter of appreciation or thank you from someone in your past who wanted to acknowledge some kindness. I know about such a letter because it happened to me.

Here is a very personal account of how I received such a letter in the most unusual of ways. My first wife, Sue, and I lost our first child at birth. A couple of years ago I was writing a memoir about my family and mentioned the story of our Anne. Over the years, I have thought about her many times, and one evening a strange thing happened as I brought her to mind. I felt a sudden and overwhelming impulse to write what was being "sent" to me. It was a letter from Anne to Sue and me explaining why she could not stay with us in the physical realm. To understand the letter better, I should add that due to some marvelous and serendipitous events, we were blessed with twin infants whom we adopted less than a month after Anne was buried.

Here is what I wrote down as it was dictated:

Dearest Mother and Father, It is now time to answer your question. At the last minute, I was called back for an urgent assignment of utmost importance. In time you will come to understand the magnitude of my calling. I can only say I helped save many lives and in that I possess a unique ability to be of service in a very specific manner. In my place I made sure you were well compensated. The two male souls were so perfect for you because I made them myself. So, in a very real way they are me and I am they, so you lost no child but gained four. I did ask my own angel guide one other thing: I would personally be available to you both, every hour of every day of your earth experiences and beyond. In your most desperate moments, I have been at your sides, supporting, protecting, and guiding. This arrangement, I assure you, is most unusual. It has been as comforting to me on my own path as it has been to you. Remember this: where you are, I have been; where you will pass, I have passed. We have been together for all eternity and we shall continue to be. So, there is no need to say hello or goodbye. There is no need to ever be fearful or sad. All is perfect just the way it is. You are blessed beyond measure, "Anne" (Lucianna)

Another example, again, in my family: Every few years my wife, Karen, a retired elementary teacher, receives from "out of the blue" a thoughtful letter from one of her students saying how she touched his or her life.

If you think back, you might have received such unexpected gifts yourself. If not, don't be surprised if you do in the not too distant future now that you have the "tomato letter" attitude.

Part Three

Crafting Your Letters

Chapter 5

The Style

I feel these letters should have immediate impact to the intended recipient. Even when he or she holds the envelope in their hands, there should be a sense of excitement, surprise, and/or anticipation. I stressed that to the doctor, and he seemed to agree since he followed my suggestions for style that I am now going to pass on to you.

Although the drafts can be written longhand or typed out, it will add to the intensity of the gift if you use special paper and write the final letter in your own hand if possible.

There are many specialty paper vendors available on the Internet as well as in office supply stores. Use a type and style that says "You" to the intended receiver. For example, I wrote some letters on a seashore motif and a couple of them on plain cream-colored paper with a dried oak leaf on the lower edge. Those stood out to me as I scanned the various stationery papers at our local office supply store. Envelopes are also very important and I always buy as close to matching ones if they don't come together.

The one I mentioned before—the banana leaf and stems—was exotic looking, but it had a rough texture that I thought might be hard to write on and hard to read. I still have some of it along with matching envelopes, so I may use them for other letters, perhaps with a Sharpie pen.

When you write your letters on exquisite sheets of paper with no lines, make sure you have some way to keep the writing straight. Unless you are an elementary school teacher, you will probably not write straight across the page. I suggest using a light table if you have access to one and place a heavy-lined paper under the sheet you are writing on. You can also use some sort of straight edge.

Whatever you use, your reader will know you took the time to make the writing straight and spaced properly.

Letting your reader see that this has taken considerable time and patience is what we are aiming for. It's similar to writing a friend a thank-you card, yet few people take the time to do that anymore. But when you get one in the mail, it speaks volumes about your friend's intentions and feelings about you and the several minutes it took. It's even more dramatic if it's a well-thought-out Tomato Letter.

Here are a few more ideas you can use in the appearance of the letter and envelope, which I shared with the doctor and which I use myself:

1. Use any size letter you want. I use the American standard size, eight and a half by eleven inches. But, different and unusual sizes may fit your personality better and make the receiver smile by the uniqueness.

2. Place it in the mail; don't hand deliver or place it in their mailbox. You are again aiming for impact, and it's always nice to receive mail. The reader will be looking it over as he or she walks

up to the house, wondering "Who is sending me this and what is it?"

3. People have told me they don't put a return address on it for added mystery, but you might consider the address but not your name. In case it doesn't reach them, you will still get it back.

4. Although I didn't think of it when I first started writing my Tomato Letters, I'm the kind of person who now considers sending them by one-day mail, for even more bang for the buck. It's not only fun to get such a mailing, but it has an immediate impact on the recipient.

5. Some people send the letter along with flowers or those edible flower bouquets popular today. I like the idea of sending it by itself so it will be the focus of the receiver's attention, but you decide.

The sky's the limit to how you seize the loved one's attention. I would caution against making the outward appearances too flashy. What we're trying to do is make the package attractive, so that they know you have taken care and time designing it, but not so loud that it takes away from the inside message.

Remember, this may be the most important message you ever communicate to your friend or loved one, so make it count.

Another thing to keep in mind is that, to the extent there are direct or indirect compliments in your letters, they will continue to occupy a special place in the recipient's heart and mind. We hardly ever forget a sincere compliment, large or small.

Why Not An Email?

Emails are the opposite of handwritten (or even typed) letters. The letters in this book are to be seen as personal, effortful, thoughtful, even "old-fashioned." Tomato Letters are also more powerful in their impact. They are unusual in this day and age. They are more likely to be saved as cherished mementos. They will be appreciated and carefully read. Emails are none of these things. Please do your best and avoid the impulse to use them in this manner.

Chapter 6

The Guidelines

When I sat back down with the doctor, I went over each of the following suggested elements with him, one by one, just as you will be reading them. I wanted him to realize this will take some time. It is to be a feeling exercise, not an analytical one.

After going through them, I asked him if he had any questions. He said he didn't, but I had given him a lot of information in just a few minutes. So, I handed him a copy of these elements or what I call the Guidelines so he could take time to reflect on them before he began writing.

The following are most of what I wrote in the short amount of time I used to type them out. Later, for my memoir-writing workshops, I added a few more. You may think of your own set of special ideas to incorporate into your letter or letters. I want to emphasize this process is intended for a generalized letter. You should feel free to particularize the list of guidelines for any of the eight types of letters as well as the specialty letters.

1. Get started right now. It's very easy to postpone this project, so start writing today. Write the first letter and you'll discover it's easier than you thought. Then proceed to the next one. Opening your heart isn't the easiest thing in the world, but you will feel good having done so.

2. Try to condense your letter to about two pages. You can write it out (or even type it) in draft form in as many pages as you like, but consider condensing it to what amounts to around ten minutes of reading or less. This will force you to include the true essence of your feelings. If you are able, writing it out in "longhand"

(cursive) will add to the importance of the letters. It's a profoundly personal touch that shows how much you care. Simply write like you talk.

3. Write your letters from a heart-to-heart consciousness. This is tough to do sometimes, so getting into the mood first really helps. I suggest reading book entries, listening to musical selections, reading poems or prayers, and/or watching a sentimental movie. A great mood song is "If Tomorrow Never Comes," sung by Garth Brooks. It could be the anthem for this book. (See the Appendix for samples of mood books, songs, poems and prayers, and movies that speak to me and hopefully to you.)

Another way to get into the mood for writing is to take advantage of the serenity and beauty nature provides us. Places like parks, ponds or lakes, nature preserves, woods, and country roads are especially helpful to me. Try these locations.

4. Composing these letters can surprise you by uncovering the depth of your personal relationship with the recipient, and bringing out your true feelings toward them. So breathe deeply and bring those feelings up onto paper. (It is said that feelings are the language of angels, so take a hint from them.)

5. Keep a copy of your letters. You will want to read these letters from time to time yourself, so keep your final draft of each. And, if your loved one makes his or her transition before you do, the letter will be a profound source of comfort.

6. Write a cover letter for sure. This is so your loved ones ease into the main letter. You want to prepare them for this most personal of letters. After all, you don't do this kind of thing for them every day, so explain *why* you are doing so. One important note I include in my cover letters is that they do not have to send me a letter in return. Of course, it would be nice if they did, but emphasize that is not the point of your letter.

7. Place in the letter nothing negative or critical. Remember, this is a loving, uplifting message from the center of your heart. This is no time for any criticism—constructive or not. After all, we've probably done enough of that throughout our relationships!

8. Take the attitude of "only ten minutes left," especially in the Last Letter category. For that one, act as if you are distilling all your thoughts and feelings to your loved one in a few brief moments. So, condense those essential feelings that you would squeeze into a few remaining minutes. I tell my workshop classes to write as if you had ten minutes to live and then you would drop dead, never to speak with your loved one again in this life. Make it that meaningful.

Central Themes for Your Letter

You may of course include anything you wish in your letters because it is *you* who knows best in such matters of the heart. But, in case you have some hesitancy or question as to content, here are some additional ideas you may consider. While aspects of these guidelines can be used for any letter, this section is especially useful for Final Letters.

1. Tell the person how much you care about him or her. This is the time for opening your heart and expressing the true extent of your love and admiration. It is the perfect time to be totally open and honest and sincere.

2. Remind the person of some poignant experiences you kept in your memory about them. Two or more examples will show the person you really cared about those times together and these instances are etched in your memory.

3. Praise this special person. Tell him or her what their best traits are, what you wished you could do that they do easily and well. Talk about their talents and their personality qualities you find admirable.

4. Say you're sorry, if appropriate. Thus, apologize for anything that you may have done to hurt them in any way, and include those things you

may have done that you don't even know about or remember, such as careless statements or omissions.

5. Thank the friend or relative. What for? For coming into your life, being an integral part of it that has helped shape you into the person you now are. Spend a few sentences extolling what this relationship has meant to you.

6. Wish them the best in life. Express your love and support for them in all their goals and aspirations, wishes, dreams and desires.

I don't know if the doctor used each of the guidelines for each of his three letters. He never showed me any of the letters and I didn't want to invade his privacy. After all, I hardly knew the man.

But I want to repeat that you can pick and choose any of the elements, although I would strongly suggest you include most of the above suggestions. It doesn't accomplish as much if you don't tell the person these things.

Chapter 7

The Presentation

There are several ways to present the letter to the loved one, depending on the circumstance. In the doctor's case he used the postal service; he simply dropped them into the mail box.

If you are estranged like the doctor was, the Internet is a valuable and ready source nowadays to find people. I use it all the time to locate them. It usually takes a matter of minutes, although sometimes it takes some additional effort.

When I wrote letters to my four sons, I called each of them and told them I was going to mail them a special letter, along with a cover letter. I asked them to read it and then to keep it in their family archives. I didn't say much more, and that in itself increases the curiosity factor. There had been no major conflicts between any of my sons and me, so it was an easy "delivery" message. You don't really even have to give the person a heads-up, but in my case I felt I wanted to.

Another method is to hand-carry the letter in an envelope to the friend or relative. If you do so, you might say something like this: "Mary, here's a letter I wrote for you. I've put down some thoughts that are easier to say in writing than in a conversation. We can discuss it afterwards. If you want to, please let me know your reaction anyway. But for now, I'll just drop it off and leave you to read it when you have about ten minutes." Then say good-bye.

Oftentimes you may be writing a letter to smooth over a long-standing problem between you and another person. For example, you and your sister may have had an intense difference of opinion about taking care of your father and it escalated into a battle. Then you broke contact for a number of years. In that situation, you might place a call to her and let her know you have put down your thoughts about that incident in a two-page letter that you will be sending her. You probably would be better off making your phone conversation short and let the letter do the talking.

In the above case, you can also consider calling your sister a few days after the letter arrives and simply ask her if she has read it and what she thought of your comments and feelings. You don't even have to do that if the relationship was strained to the point of breakage. It may be better to let your ideas within the letter incubate for a few weeks. After all, it took years of bad feelings to get to this point; it may take some time for it to do the good you had intended.

There is no guarantee your sister will contact you. But that's not the point. The letter is primarily intended to help you get over the situation. You poured out your soul and that's the most you can do.

Part Four

Your Impact

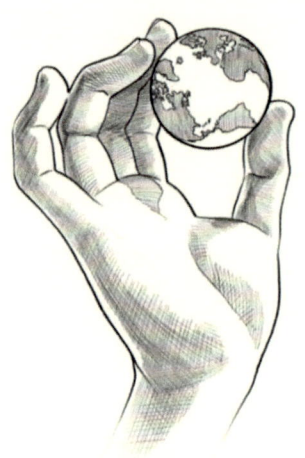

Chapter 8

Changing the World

My goal in writing this book is to change the world one letter at a time.

After I showed the doctor how to write his letters, I wanted to hurry and write my own to the people I loved most in my life as I already shared with you. So I followed my own advice and wrote my wife, my children and my mother.

I also introduced the Tomato Letters into my workshops on writing memoirs and family histories. I explain the story of the farmer and the doctor. I suggest to my participants that they go home and do the same.

I end that section of the workshop by explaining that my ultimate hope is to have one hundred thousand people write these letters. Perhaps it can grow to a million. Whatever the number, Tomato Letters can bring peace of mind and smiles to the people who matter most to all of us. They are also a wonderful legacy that can be carried down generations to our future families.

Wouldn't it be magnificent if the practice carried on and spread all over the world? In this age of Internet and social media, it's not at all unlikely when something goes "viral," right? On my website, people can list their names if they wish and the number of letters (and their categories), so it should be easy to keep track of the number. The site is also used for people to share their stories, like those of the farmer and doctor, some of which I hope to include in future book installments similar to those in the *Chicken Soup for the Soul* series.

Chapter 9

Bringing Families Together

Your letters can help soothe some family strife or heal a serious fracture that has occurred in your family somewhere down the line. For example, a long time ago there was a rift in my own family that I handled quite poorly.

There was a disagreement over a family matter between my wife and her brother that grew into a fairly substantial sore between them and eventually between my wife and me. I felt my mother-in-law sided unfairly with her son, so I eventually cut off ties with her and used my children against her, by not allowing them to receive Christmas and birthday presents from her.

Although I can't even recall much about the substance of the disagreement, I do recall when my then wife sat me down on the bed one evening and asked, in a very loving way, for me to drop the whole matter and allow our children's grandmother to give them presents. I was so intractable and full of myself that I quickly cut off the discussion with a firm "No." Fortunately, my behavior lasted only for a year, but feelings were hurt.

Some years later, when I came to my senses and matured, I wrote an apology letter to my mother-in-law, who was by then in her eighties. I explained how wrong I had been and told her how sorry I was for my crazy behavior and asked her to forgive me. She responded with a very kind letter of her own, saying she appreciated my apology and that she did in fact forgive me. She even followed up with a phone call and we talked for about ten minutes.

Even though I am still embarrassed at my smallness in that matter, I use this as an example of how a letter can heal family wounds.

The doctor's story is another excellent example of a major family healing, which will soon be revealed in Chapter 11. Many families have difficulties, many less extreme than the doctor's and some even more serious. If you have such family issues or know someone who does, you might give them a copy of this book.

Chapter 10

Brightening Your Star

The Galilean talked more than once about letting your light shine and that "You are the light of the world." Among other things, I believe He meant that our inner nature is ready to display our transcendent love in any manner of circumstances.

One such way to let our own light shine is when we open our hearts and minds through letter writing that gives others a demonstration of our divine nature. I think of people who are terribly sad, angry or antagonistic as having closed hearts. My analogy is like having one's heart (soul) closed tight like a camera's lens aperture that stops all light from entering. When it begins to open, even slightly, light races in and begins to heal the person.

It is an act of that same love when you take the time and effort to release yourself from the human tendency to hide your true feelings and, instead, go all out to expose those thoughts and feelings of your higher self to those who will benefit greatly from them.

Who knows, you might send off your letter or letters at the precise time when the friend or relative is in greatest need to receive it. That is, in fact, how such things often work.

One impressive impact of writing healing letters is definitely on you, the writer, who takes the initiative. First, it releases you from the shackles of guilt or postponement or abandonment you may have had before, sometimes for many years. Second, the act of sitting down and writing can recreate or improve a relationship that had been closed off. But, mostly, it allows you the freedom to move on. What price can you put on that?

Writing also may have the unexpected result of unleashing a cascade of letters from the receiver to another receiver and on and on, perhaps around the world as is my goal.

You will be a better, freer person for having spent an hour or two letting one human know you care enough about him or her, with this unusual blessing.

Part Five

The Rest of the Story

Chapter 11

The Miracle

Surprisingly, I never gave much thought to the doctor and his assignment until later that fall, when I passed by his duplex and thought of my unusual encounter with him. I did think of those eight delicious tomatoes several times.

One day in November I was in his neighborhood and decided to see how he was getting along. I was sure he didn't write those letters. But, even if he didn't, I liked him and wanted to chat with him again. I might even be able to urge him on to complete his project.

The doctor greeted me as an old friend. He shook hands with me in his professional demeanor, then came right out and said, "I have some fantastic news for you. Come right in!"

"I took your advice and composed each letter separately. I completed all of them within three days and mailed them off. You know what? Within several weeks, my friend, I got calls from my former wife and both boys. It's like a miracle!"

I was speechless and amazed he wrote the letters in the first place, and I was even more surprised that his family responded. After all, it had been many years of estrangement with no word at all between them.

He spent an hour telling me what they said. They appreciated his thorough letter-writing, which was totally out of character for the man they had known. He agreed with them that his former self would never have considered such a bold move or such a heartwarming attitude. He confessed he used to be a terrible father to the boys, always pushing them to accomplish more in a critical way, and the same with his wife, whom he had continually berated.

I remember on our first visit, when he asked for my help in composing the letters, he said he was going to tell one boy how lazy he had been in putting off applying for college. I broke him off in the middle of his tirade. "Doctor," I told him, "that's exactly what *not* to put in your conciliatory letter. That's the man they ran away from!" He must have taken that to heart or else they would never have contacted him.

I was elated for him: He seemed ten years younger, happier and thankful for my help. I didn't pursue how they would all proceed from there. I figured it would be a slow process for complete forgiveness. As a psychiatrist, he knew that better than I.

I left contented that my small contribution helped push him forward. I never saw him after that. However, I used that letter structure for my own family, incorporated it into my workshops, and now have told the story in this book.

Chapter 12

The Mystery

It's been years since I finally picked up my notes and resumed writing this book about the farmer and the doctor. After writing the second draft a few months ago, I decided to look up the doctor's name and contact any remaining family members to try to understand how their relationships had healed.

I drove past the home where I first called on him. I wasn't sure of the exact place, but I narrowed it down to one of two duplexes on the short street. I wrote down the addresses so I could look up his name at the local library. I remembered the approximate time frame and consulted those two street directories by year. No Lithuanian-sounding name came up at either of the addresses. I even expanded the addresses, but still no luck.

I next called up several psychiatrists and psychologists in the area who would have been around when he practiced in the 1970s and 1980s. No one had ever heard of such a person as I described him. I then called the local hospitals where he would have had seen patients, with the same results. It was as if he disappeared and erased every trace of his life in town.

Could I have been mistaken about where I had twice visited him? Could I have gotten his nationality wrong? Or his being a psychiatrist? No. I have a very good memory, many of my friends and relatives tell me, after reading several of my memoirs. (When describing our next-door neighbor, one childhood friend surprised me by saying, "You remember more things about my dad than I do!")

Did I make the whole thing up in my mind? It was feeling a little like I was in an episode of "The Twilight Zone," so I asked my wife if she remembered the day I wrote the outline for those appreciation letters and showed her a copy that same afternoon when she came home from school. She did remember and reminded me that I had excitedly recounted the story that very day it happened. "In fact, Ken, I asked you where you got those tomatoes; we had some in our salads that night."

So it seems this story ends as unexpectedly as it began. Maybe that's how all stories should be.

Conclusion

I wish I had had the presence of mind to stay in touch with the farmer as well as the doctor, but their lives went on and mine did too. I was busy earning a living and filling the rest of the day with common activities.

These two men whom I ran into "accidentally" played a key role in my life—and yours too, if you accept the challenge to write your own Tomato Letters. If this story is any indication, we meet those in life we are supposed to meet. We can take from them something as important as I did or, in some cases, we give them something.

That reminds me of the time I was exasperated at my biology classes when Joe, a fellow science teacher enlightened me, "Ken, something you say to a student in kindness today may come back to him or her years later. You never know how you touch their lives." Over the eight years as a teacher I have tried to offer to many students words of encouragement and optimism. Sometimes, just listening was enough, I'd like to think.

That's what I'm hoping for in this book: that you and those you send your letters to will feel better for having connected heart to heart. And, if you and I are really lucky, subsequent letters will continue to multiply.

Now, go and write them and then let me know how it turns out.

Author's Note

More Eight Tomato Stories and Letters?

Some of the stories and examples of letters in this book are from people just like you. If you have stories and letters you would like to submit, please send them to us at the address below. We may choose yours in another related book, so please send them in.

Thank you.

Eight Tomatoes

Website: http:// www. KenMitchellBooks.com

Appendix

To Whom Should I Write?

Throughout this book, I have laid out ideas to whom you might want to write your letters. In addition to these thought starters, there are some obvious people to choose first: the sister-in-law you had words with that fractured your relationship, the friend at work you felt moved in front of you for that promotion, that neighbor who placed his fence a foot onto your property.

If you are having trouble thinking where to start, here is a list of possible candidates for your heartfelt letters.

1. Parents
2. Siblings
3. Aunts and uncles
4. Cousins
5. Grandparents and great-grandparents
6. In-laws
7. Neighbors in your adult years
8. Neighbor children you grew up with
9. Schoolmates
10. Teachers
11. Fellow workers
12. Supervisors

13. Employees
14. Business partners
15. Business associates
16. Your own children
17. Your children's friends
18. Your children's friends' parents
19. Close friends, past or present
20. People in your social groups
21. Your repairmen
22. Your contractors
23. People you purchase things from
24. People who buy things from you
25. Your doctor(s), dentist, chiropractor, et al.
26. Friends with whom you play sports
27. Social friends
28. People with whom you share hobbies
29. People you dated
30. Lovers
31. Former spouses/partners
32. Church associates
33. A stranger you met
34. A pet
35. A kindred spirit

Some Topics You Might Cover

Here are some ideas you might encounter in your life journey that could benefit from sending off a letter to just the right person. These are random in that they are not listed in the order of letter categories in Part 2 of this book.

- To a homeless person asking for help on a street corner, advising how to get back on track
- To a niece who recently needed rehab in an addiction center, wishing best luck in her recovery
- To a stranger whose newspaper story of overcoming caught your eye, congratulating them
- To your neighbor who won a lottery, encouraging them to remember those who need help and also congratulating them
- To your physician assistant, thanking her for her kindness and time in answering all of your questions
- To your spouse during a turbulent time straightening out a family squabble on his/her side, for keeping even keeled and especially his sense of humor in your household

- To your guardian angel asking her to "talk" to an old friend of yours in solving a spat between him/her and you.
- To an elected office holder, thanking her for pushing for a difficult compromise at the city council meeting
- To one of your child's teachers, appreciating his special guidance and extra time
- To a great-aunt with whom you lost contact, opening a dialogue for ways to connect
- To a pet who had to be put to sleep, expressing your affection for her company over the years and missing her deeply
- To the president of a foods company, thanking him and his employees for the fine quality product your family has enjoyed
- To a long-lost friend, saying how sorry you are for letting that misunderstanding break your bond and wishing to reunite
- To a high school best friend for being there for you during those adolescent days, especially all those late-night phone calls
- To your softball coach for benching you when you became unglued in that one game, teaching you self-control

Mood Reading Selections

The Bible, King James Version, 1611

Discover the Power Within You: A Guide to the Unexplored Depths Within, Eric Butterworth, 1992, HarperCollins

How Then Shall We Live?: Four Simple Questions That Reveal the Beauty and Meaning of Our Lives, Wayne Muller, 1996, Bantam Books

The Prophet, Kahlil Gibran, 1923, Alfred A. Knopf

Ordinary People As Monks and Mystics: Lifestyles for Self-discovery, Marsha Sinetar, 1986, Paulist Press

You Can Have It All: A Simple Guide to a Joyful and Abundant Life, Arnold M. Patent, 1995, Pocket Books

"Our Town," Thornton Wilder, 1938

As a Man Thinketh, James Allen, 1903, Various Publishers

Illusions: The Adventures of a Reluctant Messiah, Richard Bach, 1977, Dell Publishing Co., Inc.

Embraced by the Light, Betty J. Eadie, 1992, Bantam Books

Spoon River Anthology, Edgar Lee Masters, 1915, Penguin Books

Mood Music Selections

"If Tomorrow Never Comes," Garth Brooks

"What a Wonderful World," Louis Armstrong

"The Prayer," Andrea Bocelli & Celine Dion

"Take My Hand, Precious Lord," Jim Reeves

"Just a Closer Walk with Thee," Patsy Cline/Willie Nelson

"Green, Green Grass of Home," Tom Jones

"Divine Gregorian Chant," instrumental by Patrick Lenk

"There Goes My Everything," Engelbert Humperdinck

"Time to Say Goodbye," Sarah Brightman & Andre Bocelli

"Somewhere Over the Rainbow," Judy Garland

"Annie's Song," John Denver

"I Have a Dream," ABBA

"Help Me Make It Through the Night," Norah Jones

"Greensleeves," The Celtic Ladies

"Stranger on the Shore," played by Acker Bilk

Mood Poems & Prayers Selections

Henry V's Speech, "We Happy Few, We Band of Brothers," recited by Kenneth Branagh

"Serenity Prayer," Dr. Reinhold Niebuhr

"If Thou Must Love Me," Elizabeth Barrett Browning

"If," Rudyard Kipling

"Invictus," Henley

"Our Deepest Fear," Marianne Williamson

"Stopping by Woods on a Snowy Evening," Robert Frost

"On Children," Khalil Gibran

"The Prophet on Death," Khalil Gibran

"When I Die," Rumi

"Don't Stand by My Grave and Weep," Mary Elizabeth Fry

"Success," Ralph Waldo Emerson

"Annabelle Lee," Edgar Allan Poe

Mood Movies Selections

"Somewhere in Time" (1980)

"Family Man," (2000)

"City of Angels," (1998)

"Cocoon," (1985)

"A Prairie Home Companion," (2006)

"It's a Wonderful Life," (1946)

"Meet Joe Black," (1998)

"Bodyguard," (1992)

"Mr. Holland's Opus," (1995)

"Romeo & Juliet," (1968)

"October Baby," (2011)

"Dead Poet's Society," (1989)

"Field of Dreams," (1989)

"NY Memories—Andre Rieu" (2020)

Cover Letter Example

Dear Gabrielle,

    I am writing you this letter to show you how much I have admired you over the years. It is something I have felt about you for a long time, and I thought I would set it down in written form in my own handwriting.

    I want to emphasize I'm not doing it for any particular reason. I am not sick or dying. I'm not moving away. I just wanted to tell you in personal terms what you have meant to me and my family.

    You do not have to respond either with a similar letter or in a conversation. I have no ulterior motives for doing so.

    The one thing I do want to mention is that if you feel it has moved you, you might consider doing the same for others whom you admire, love and respect.

    The continued best to you.

        Your friend,

Appreciation/Gratitude/ Congratulations Letter Example

March 8, 1996

Dear [Son],

I've been wanting to write this letter for a long, long time. Now that I'm in Haiti, I finally have the time to do it and do it right. I'll type it on my computer when I get home and then send it to you.

While all of this is fresh in my mind, I want to tell you a few things that you deserve to hear. I think everyone in your mom's family and my family are so happy for you and proud of you for wanting to be a medical doctor. . .

. . . Many times I think how much I would have liked to graduate from college. I know this had been a concern of mine during most of my whole work life. Fortunately, it worked out fairly well for me. I envy you, at times, for following through and doing what you know is important. Many of your friends, who are having a good time now, may be sorry later for not furthering their education. You shouldn't ever have to worry about or wonder where you will be working. You'll probably be able to pick and choose your type of work and location.

My only hope is that you will not forget or stray from your Christian training. I guess I would rather have you a poor penniless Christian child of God than a rich doctor who has fallen away from your faith. My dad set a good example for me by attending church every Sunday when possible, and I've been trying to do the same for you. I know you have been very busy during the last number of years, and I'm sure you'll get back to attending church regularly very soon. Right? Don't wait till you're rich and famous, it'll be too difficult then. The people I admire most at church are the medical doctors. They seem to have it all together and seem to be very happy. . .

Again, I do want to say I'm happy for you and want you to know I realize how hard you've worked to get this far. I think about that a lot.

Love you always,

Dad

Love Letter Example

Dear Anne,

Today marks a big event in your life.
        Yes, my daughter, it's your 21st!
Only, your first breath never taken—such a strife.
        You were lost before I knew you—What a curse!

But as I look back over these 21 years,
        I imagine what you would have been.
Yes, today we would have celebrated with beers
        And even laughed at your first taste of gin.

I know you would have been the big sis—
        Just like an ole mother hen.

All these years we have talked about you.
        You were beautiful, kind, charming and smart!
Your first Prom dress would have been a heavenly blue.
        You were so tomboyish, so squeamish and so tart.

You have become for us our guardian angel—our very own!
        We felt so special every time we visited the grave.

We still wondered, "Why didn't she breathe when born?"
>   But with you high above, your brothers felt safe and brave.

There are no candles to light
>   Because you have only lived in the tomb.

No party favors, no hats or cake to bite
>   Because you are a flower that never bloom'd.

>   Love,
>   Your Mother

A Forgiving Letter Example

Dear Frank,

    You were right when you told me over the phone that I could not prove that you had stolen the corn from me. My father-in-law and I asked an attorney if I had a chance of winning a lawsuit, and he said it would be difficult to prove in cases like this . . . .

    . . . Still, Frank, I have decided to let all this go between us. I do so more as a practical matter. You see, I don't want that negativity to eat at me for years to come. . . .

    So, I forgive you for the choice you made that season and hope you have come to a principled understanding of your wrongdoing. While I thought I really needed that money for the rest of the down payment on the land, I was able to come up with it in the end. I guess all's well that ends well.

    I must confess that my forgiving you took some time. I went through the feelings of anger and betrayal—

all that kind of stuff. But in the end, I feel good about getting those feelings off my chest.

Here's hoping you are doing well, and you and your family enjoy a wonderful life together.

Blessings,

Apology/Asking for Forgiveness/ I'm Sorry Letter Example

Dear Ed,

I owe you a long overdue apology. Knowing you, I'm sure you have forgotten all about it since it was many years ago. But, it has been something I feel I owe you and I haven't forgotten.

When you lost your farm and had to have a farm sale, your many friends came over to help you move all the equipment and miscellaneous farm items to get ready for the auction.

My wife asked me that Saturday morning, "Aren't you going to help Ed with the farm sale? The other guys are already over there."

I told her no and explained that it was too sad an affair and I'd rather just stay away. She then reminded me how you would drop whatever you were doing and come help me on my farm whenever I asked. You did that multiple times, I reminded myself. You were a good friend that way.

Moreover, our families were also very close. Our kids played together and our wives were good friends.

However, I apparently had put all that out of my mind that day. I just stayed away when you and the others were moving things out of the barns and into the field for the sale.

It was small of me to stay away, and I am ashamed I was absent when you needed me. I want to apology for being so thoughtless to a good friend who was always helping me.

I know such a belated "sorry" doesn't seem like much. But I do feel you deserve to have me at least recognize I did wrong. Here's hoping you will accept it.

I am happy that your life after farming has been so successful, and you and Joan have raised four happy, healthy children and are now enjoying a nice retirement. Here's to many more years!

Sincerely,

Thank You Letter Example

Dear Bob,

It was a surprise, along with a deep sense of gratitude, when I received your gift in the mail today.

When I begin any writing project, I feel the right people will come into my life to fill in the skill gaps. It has happened in each of my career moves and it has happened in my writing life . . .

. . . Now, when I was trying to figure out how to cover the major cost of printing the first edition of my newest book, you send me this stipend.

I cannot thank you enough, Bob, for your support. You are indeed a friend who sees value in my work and for that I am eternally grateful.

I had a wonderful time with you and your sister at dinner last week. It was so thoughtful of you to make a point of contacting me when you came to town. Until we meet again.

Blessings,

Sympathy/Condolences Letter Example

Executive Mansion
Washington, Nov. 21, 1864.

Dear Madam,

I have been shown in the files of the War Department a statement of the Adjutant General of Massachusetts that you are the mother of five sons who have died gloriously on the field of battle.

I feel how weak and fruitless must be any words of mine which should attempt to beguile you from the grief of a loss so overwhelming. But I cannot refrain from tendering to you the consolation that may be found in the thanks of the Republic they died to save.

I pray that our Heavenly Father may assuage the anguish of your bereavement, and leave you only the cherished memory of the loved and lost, and the solemn pride that must be yours to have laid so costly a sacrifice upon the altar of Freedom.

Yours, very sincerely and respectfully,

A. Lincoln.

[To] Mrs. Bixby.

Advising Letter Example

Dear [Prospective Employer],

 I have known Jillian [Last Name] for several years. I was one of her teachers at [Name] High School, and I also hired her to assist me in my writing business. She is one of those rare people who seems to have it all—personality, work ethic, brains, and a maturity beyond her years.

 In school, Jillian was the kind of student who kept her head down and worked hard. In her yearbook class, she was one of the main editors and knew how to organize, cooperate and meet production schedules. She was one of the top students in her graduating class—fourth if I recall correctly. She was also liked by everybody—staff, teachers and fellow students . . .

 Do yourself a favor: give her an interview and job offer before someone else snatches this talented young lady. You'll be happy you did. It will make you and the college look good.

    Yours Truly,

The Last Letters/Saying Goodbye Letter Example

Dear Mom,

When I think back on my life with you, I bring back so many happy memories that make me smile.

I remember the warmth of a caring mother who stayed up countless nights when I was sick. You set up the steam inhaler with the sheet over my head so I could breathe easier. You swabbed my throat when I was bleeding after tonsil surgery, and you rushed me to the hospital when I cut my lip that time . . .

You helped me reach my independence in many ways. The day you put me on the city bus by myself to go downtown. That was both scary and reassuring, after all those many trips we took together on that familiar bus route . . .

You and Dad always encouraged me to study hard and improve myself. Like the many evenings at the kitchen table when you helped Cindy and me do our homework. You would patiently help us as long as we needed help . . .

It was fun when you and I went hunting for leaves and insects for my biology class collections. Remember when we came up on that big bull snake that scared the wits out of us? . . .

Another thing I always felt good about was how you and Dad would be at every game I would play at the park. It was comforting seeing you up in the stands as I came up to bat. And you and Dad were instrumental in raising money for the park . . .

You have been an extraordinary wife too. Always helping Dad with finances and working to earn extra money. But, especially being the good nurse when he grew old and needed your help the most. He appreciated it and Cindy and I felt good knowing you were taking care of him . . .

You should feel proud of your life so far. From growing up to becoming a nurse to being a housewife in the fifties, and now your retirement years. It's been a great ride and you are still young at heart and ready to enter a new century. And the best is yet to come!

Thanks, Mom. Love you.

Angel Letter Example

Dear Angel of Joe,

    I have been at a loss to understand why Joe has not responded to any of my many requests to finish my kitchen renovation. I don't think I said or did anything wrong. This is so upsetting to me because I have paid him up to date for his work and even a little beyond.

    I don't know much about the law in such matters. I don't know if I can hire another contractor to complete the work? Or if Joe would still have a lien on my house? And, I don't want to talk with an attorney.

    Can you please intervene and somehow convince Joe to come back and finish the work or at least contact me to let me know what I should do?

    I have always had good relationships with people and consider myself a caring and nice person. For the life of me, I can't figure out what I have done, if anything. Hope to hear from Joe soon. Thank you.

Letter to God Example

Dear God,

I am writing to you because I do not know where else to turn. I feel like Job must have felt. I have tried to live a good and decent life, but the world is coming down on me.

I have diabetes, a daughter with a serious disability, an alcoholic husband, and I just lost my job. I would seriously consider calling it quits altogether, but Jane needs me more than ever.

I can hardly sleep at night with this crushing stress on me. I don't talk with my mother or sister about my problems. It's difficult to confide in anybody. I've always been a reserved person and find it almost impossible to ask others for help or even show my true feelings.

I've been a Christian all my life, but I am at a total loss. I suppose I have depression because I seem to be able to accomplish nothing. I should be looking for a job but I don't seem to know where to start.

Please, if you hear me, come to my aid. I am so desperate. Thank you.

Letter to Your Future Family Example

March 10, 2020

Dear member of my future [name] family,

I am writing you in the hopes this letter will make it through time and space to our future generations. I hope it will let you know a little about me, your distant-grandfather, or some other relative way back in 2020. My goal is to have you and other descendants of mine read this at least seven generations into the future from my time.

I would have greatly enjoyed receiving such a letter from kin back seven generations, possibly from a man or woman who lived around 1850. Some families actually have letters or diaries from such forebearers that long ago, even longer. This is in the hope you will actually be the beneficiary of such a letter.

Sit down and make yourself a cup of tea because this is a long letter. I will include something of my family, my career, challenges I've had along the way, and some personal insights that may be advantageous for you and your family and your future family as well . . .

. . . I hope you have gotten to know me after reading about my life and thoughts. I am a writer in my later years and I have written several family biographies as well as several memoirs. Hopefully, these will have been preserved in our family archives. If not, I have sent copies of them to the Illinois State Historical Library (as well as my local library) for safekeeping. If for some reason they are lost to the world, this letter will serve to let you know a little about me and my family in our era.

I will ask you to consider writing a similar letter to your (and my) future family and to keep this tradition going for as long as possible.

Here's wishing you the best in your life.

[First, Middle & Last Name]
[Complete Address & Country]

Letter to a Child Example

Dear Saul,

    I only have one grandchild, but that has been enough. You are wonderful, smart, reverent and a joy to have seen you grow up through middle school.

    You have shown valor in overcoming many obstacles in your young life. You have never felt sorry for yourself, as far as I could see, for the cards you have been dealt. Most people, whether young or old, would not have reacted to adversity as well as you.

    When your parents died in that awful accident, you were spared. Even though you carry those injuries with you, you decided not to let them control your life and make you feel sorry for yourself.

    It is a further commentary on your character that, after years of rehabilitation, you rose above that challenge to study hard and persevere when others with lesser will would have folded. Graduating first in your eighth-grade class made my heart swell with pride.

I'm sure you will do the same as you progress through high school next year, then college, and later medical school to obtain your PhD in your chosen field of immunology research.

Saul, you have that unquenchable spirit that raises you head and shoulders above the rest.

Continue growing in mind and spirit and great things will be in store for you.

With devotion and love,

Your grandfather

Letter to a Deceased Relative or Friend Example

Dear John,

I have decided to write you more than 20 years after you passed away. I've actually been meaning to write to you since shortly after your transition, but my only excuse is that life got in the way.

You were my first boss, my mentor for college and our fraternity, and the best man in my wedding. Yet, over the years, our paths pretty much moved away from each other.

I can't even think of the last time we saw each other. It may have been when you were in the hospital. But I may have made that up in my mind. I'm not sure.

What I am sure about is that I owe you a lot. That's why you enjoy a prominent place on My Wall of Gratitude in my office.

From your keeping part of my paycheck so I could receive weekly "running money" checks at [college name], to giving me that hundred dollar bill when I graduated and telling me it was for my "prosperity consciousness." (I did keep it in my wallet for several years before spending it!)

Those were good deeds you did, Brother John.

I was amazed you woke up so early to attend my initiation into our beloved fraternity which began at sunrise. I know that was a sacrifice, but you were there for me.

You talked so often about Judy Garland, your favorite singer, that I came to listen to her in my later years. I now share your taste in her singing. Thank you.

My suspicion is that you have been following my life arc from your vantage point. If so, you know I became a writer of sorts. All the time I spent researching our fraternity's early history and recording it, I was thinking, "John, you should be the one writing this book." You probably would have smiled if I said that, right?

Thanks for being a good friend, a big brother, and a fraternity brother—all rolled up in one.

All the best to you . . . and much gratitude!

Time-Release Letter Example

[Future Date]

Dearest [Daughter],

    I can't believe it! You are today a half century old. Congratulations! If I were alive today, I would be 105—that's what happens when parents have children later in life. But having you was a total joy. We could not have chosen a better daughter. You were as near perfect as they come.

    Your mother and I were fortunate to be with you for as many years as we had. We were able to raise you, go to your ballgames and attend your graduations. We helped you move into your own home. We were also there when you secured your first job. All great memories I will enjoy for eternity.

    I was always in prideful wonder how you took to saving money, not a strength of mine. You were a natural at being a good steward with your finances—something most people never achieve. Why, you had three different savings accounts shortly after college. By now, I am confident you have crossed that rare threshold of being a millionaire. I guess I am most proud that you never took on a penny of debt. Bravo to you!

Well, by this time in your life—on this red- letter date—you have figured out and mastered life, probably as well as anyone. I hope you have had a good life since our leaving: good health, good relationships, good careers. Most of all, good service to others on their travels through this earth experience. Remember, we're all in this together.

Until my next letter or until we meet again in the next life, God bless and be good and enjoy yourself.

Love,

Dad

Letter to Your Self Example

Dear Self,

Well, here goes another letter. It seems I write you whenever I think of my many acts of not doing the right thing or doing nothing when I should have acted. I have written to you in my diary from time to time, but I haven't been the best of diarists now, have I?

Here's to say I owe myself—you—some slack because I am often my own worst critic. Lately, I have been putting things off. I probably do ten times more activities than the average man my age, but I still am wanting to accomplish more. Is that a virtue or a vice?

I needed to write to you because I don't always know what the right thing is to do. You'd think by now I'd have that figured out. It's like all the other mysteries of life I thought I would have solved by now. Little did I know that things get fuzzier, not clearer, as one gets older.

Anyway, I needed a break and wanted to connect with you. I feel better that I've "talked" with someone, so I'll get back to work.

Have a good day, Old Friend.

Kenneth C. Mitchell

About the Author

Ken Mitchell is an author, workshop leader and speaker. His books have been published through his own company, Seagull Press. Some of his books are available on his personal website, www.KenMitchellBooks.com.

He began his writing career with biographies of his parents. Mitchell has also written several memoirs and local histories, including *North-End Pride: The History of Lanphier High School, Its People and Community* (2015), which continues to be a local best-seller in the Springfield, IL area.

Ken earned a B.A. in history from Millikin University in Decatur, IL and a B.S. in biology and education from the University of Illinois—Springfield. He has had a range of interesting careers, most of them having sales and marketing as the common threads. His avocations include aviation (he is a licensed pilot), history of religions, tennis, and sports cars.

Ken lives in Springfield, IL with his wife, Karen Kelly, a retired first-grade teacher, and their daughter, Zem. Ken also has four sons from his first marriage, Robb (Sue), Todd (Tracy), Brett, and Ladd (Emily), and five grandchildren, Brody, Tegan, Audree, Simon and Calliope. Their Australian Shepherd ("Shep") and tabby cat ("Mr. Mittens") round out their family.

Ken continues to write tomato letters.

To Order

This or Other Books by the Author

Call Our Office at

217-787-7100

or go to

www.KenMitchellBooks.com

PayPal or Major Credit Cards

Ask about special discounts

for bulk purchases

 **Seagull Press**

Publishing • Editing • Consulting • Speaking • Seminars

Notes

Notes

Notes

Notes

Notes